A SONGBIRD DREAMS OF SINGING

Animal poems to share at bedtime

written by
KATE HOSFORD

illustrated by
JENNIFER M. POTTER

PUFFIN

For Autumn

PUFFIN BOOKS

UK | USA | Canada | Ireland | Australia
India | New Zealand | South Africa

Puffin Books is part of the Penguin Random House group of companies
whose addresses can be found at global.penguinrandomhouse.com.

www.penguin.co.uk
www.puffin.co.uk
www.ladybird.co.uk

 Penguin
Random House
UK

Published in the United States by Running Press Kids,
an imprint of Perseus Books LLC,
a subsidiary of Hachette Book Group Inc. 2019
Published in Great Britain by Puffin Books 2019

001

Printed in Italy

A CIP catalogue record for this book is available from the British Library

ISBN: 978–0–241–42111–6

All correspondence to:
Puffin Books, Penguin Random House Children's, 80 Strand, London WC2R 0RL

A NOTE FROM THE AUTHOR

Did you know humans are able to survive longer without food than they can without sleep? This rest time is so essential that people who get very little sleep each night are more likely to have health problems and live shorter lives. Infants need a great deal of sleep for normal brain development, and as we get older, we still need a lot of sleep to function properly. Given these facts, it is probably not surprising to learn that most of us will spend up to a third of our lives asleep.

Sleep isn't just essential for humans, but for all animals. Although scientists are still unsure exactly why we need sleep, there are many theories. One is that sleep helps the brain repair different systems in the body, such as the immune, circulatory, and metabolic systems. Sleep may also be a time when the brain sorts through memories and decides which to keep and which to throw out. Another theory is that sleep allows our brain cells to repair themselves and recover from the day. It's likely that sleep does not have a single purpose, but rather helps in many ways at once. Some research suggests that even animals without brains might sleep, like the jellyfish, who has only a simple set of nerve cells spread throughout her body. If this is true, perhaps there are even more basic reasons why sleep evolved, like the need to conserve energy. Whatever its function, sleep also seems to be necessary for very simple nervous systems.

In the animal kingdom, there is a huge range in the amount of sleep different animals need. The sperm whale may be able to get by on as little as an hour and a half per day, while the koala sleeps up to twenty-two hours a day. Because many animals do not have one uninterrupted sleep period like we do, the length of each "nap" can also vary. For example, worker fire ants sleep for a minute at a time, while giraffes may take five-minute naps, and lions may nap for five hours at a time. Although hibernation is a different state from sleep, bears may hibernate for up to seven months and snails may rest for up to three years! Still other animals – like dolphins and ducks – sleep with only half of their brain at a time, allowing them to rest while remaining on the lookout for predators.

When different animals sleep also varies. Diurnal animals – like sea otters and ducks – are active during the day and sleep at night. Nocturnal animals – like two-toed sloths and spring peepers – are active during the night and sleep during the day. Crepuscular animals, such as the ocelot, are most active during the hours of dawn and dusk, while cathemeral animals – like some species of lemurs – have active periods during both day and night.

Why do the sleep habits of animals vary so greatly? We can apply a few general rules that are usually true: animals who sleep in a safe place tend to sleep longer. Animals who do not have to worry about predators can afford to slumber more, and animals who do not have to work as hard to find food also have more time to sleep.

In the pages that follow, you'll learn that animals sleep in a variety of positions: upside down, standing on one leg, holding hands, while swimming, and even while flying! You will also learn that some animals are capable of dreaming. While there is still much to learn as scientists continue their research, I hope you find the sleep habits of animals as fascinating as the animals themselves.

THE MYSTERIOUS SLEEP OF
MOTHER WHALES

Oh mighty mothers of the sea
Why do you slumber vertically?
Your sleep is very short it seems
But do you have gigantic dreams?

(How lovely, drifting
Through the deep
While also drifting
Off to sleep.)

Oh sleeping giants, tell us why
So many of you face the sky?
While others like to turn around
And sleep with noses facing down?

(How lovely, drifting
Through the deep
While also drifting
Off to sleep.)

Majestic creatures down below,
What other secrets do you know?
Perhaps they're meant for you to keep
While drifting, drifting
Off to sleep.

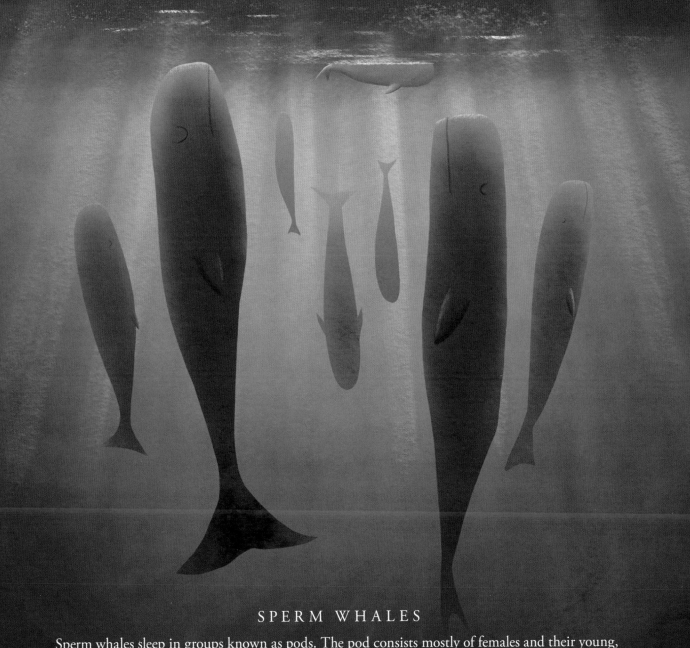

SPERM WHALES

Sperm whales sleep in groups known as pods. The pod consists mostly of females and their young, who float on the surface of the ocean while their mothers sleep vertically. (When they are not breeding, male adult sperm whales live on their own.) Although the sleeping habits of whales need to be studied further, scientists estimate that they sleep only one and a half hours a day – less than any other mammal.

These mysterious whales have two vertical sleeping positions: tail-down and nose-down. We are not sure why sperm whales sleep vertically; it might be because they are relaxing their muscles. Once they are fully relaxed, they will drift into a tail-down position because their tails weigh more than their heads. The whales that slumber nose-down dive downward to begin their rest, but eventually drift to the tail-down position when they are fully relaxed. This state of full relaxation keeps animals who have REM (rapid eye movement) sleep from acting out their dreams. It is therefore possible that sperm whales experience REM sleep and dream.

WHY THE GIRAFFE TAKES TINY NAPS

Here's the deal.
A giraffe
Doesn't want to
Be a meal.

But the trees
In the savannah
Can't begin
To conceal

This extraordinary
Animal
Whose stature
Is unreal.

If a cackle of
Hyenas should happen
To steal

Across the
Savannah,

Then it
Would be ideal
If this giraffe were
Wide awake
So she can try
To make
A break.

A tiny nap is all
she'll take.

More would be
A big mistake.

GIRAFFES

On average, giraffes sleep for about four and a half hours a night, but in short naps, each one lasting between five and eleven minutes. There are a couple of reasons they must remain constantly alert. The savannahs, where the giraffes often live, are open grasslands with trees that cannot conceal them. Also, once giraffes are lying down, it takes them a very long time to stand up again, which means they could become the next meal for a hungry lion or a group of hyenas. While the most common sleeping position for an adult giraffe is standing up fully, they sometimes rest their heads on their rumps or lie down for a few minutes and sleep, often with one eye open. Because they are protected by their parents, baby giraffes can afford to lie down and sleep curled up like a pretzel.

TREES ARE WHERE
THE LIONS LIE

Trees are where the lions lie
When hiding from the tsetse fly
Or from the angry buffalo
Who grumble on the ground below.

Trees are where the lions drape
Their bodies in a graceful shape.
But sadly, larger males cannot
Slumber in this special spot.

Lions sleeping in the trees
Are cooled when wind
runs through the leaves.
If nursing mothers need a break,
A nap in trees is what they'll take.

When all the flies have flown away
And buffalo begin to stray,
Then lions usually can be found
Sleeping soundly on the ground.

LIONS

Although lions usually sleep on the ground in the shade of trees, females and their young will sometimes sleep in trees to avoid insects or buffalo. The trees may also allow them to spot prey and enjoy the breeze. Nursing mothers will sometimes sleep in trees to take a break from their cubs. Male lions can rest up to twenty hours a day, spending ten to fifteen hours of that time sleeping. The females, who do most of the hunting, sleep less. Because wrestling down large animals takes a lot of energy, and because lions do not eat every day, it is important that they sleep between hunts. Also, lions have a great deal of muscle that they can only cool down through rest or sleep.

MOTHER OTTER
GIVES ADVICE TO HER PUP

Sleeping otter, swirling sea,
Be careful not to float away.

Hold my hand – stay close to me,
Sleeping otter, swirling sea.

This kelp, so long and tangly
Will help you not to go astray.

Sleeping otter, swirling sea,
Be careful not to float away!

SEA OTTERS

Sea otters are diurnal animals who are active during the day and sleep at night. While some sea otters sleep on land, most sleep in the ocean while floating on their backs. In order not to float away from each other, they will sometimes hold hands and wrap themselves in kelp. Sea otters have several features that make sleeping in the water comfortable: water-repellent fur, which keeps them warm and dry; webbed feet; and nostrils and ears that are able to close to keep out the water.

OH, TO BE A CHIMPANZEE!

When the sun is shining brightly
She will swing from tree to tree,
Grasping at the branches tightly.
Oh, to be a chimpanzee!

A luscious fig, or juicy flea
She will find and share politely
With a friend or two or three.

She'll build a nest for sleeping, nightly
High, where she won't have to flee
From leopards who are stepping lightly.
Oh, to be a chimpanzee!

CHIMPANZEES

Chimpanzees sleep for about nine hours a night. Each day, they find a sturdy tree with two strong branches and make a new sleep nest out of leaves and twigs. Sometimes chimps will even make a pillow out of some of the softest leaves. These sleeping nests keep them safe from predators. While chimps are very social animals, they will almost always sleep alone; the only exception is when a mother is nursing her young. Although chimps are usually active during the day, they can also be active on moonlit nights.

WHAT THE OCELOT
WAS TAUGHT

His mother taught the ocelot
That during daylight hours he ought
To sleep in leaves and trees a lot
Where he is hard to spot.

She also taught the ocelot
To hunt at dawn and dusk a lot
When it is often not as hot
And he is hard to spot.

But if the ocelot forgot
The lessons that his mother taught –
Or if it were an afterthought
To sleep in leaves and trees a lot,

And hunt when he is hard to spot,
And do exactly as he ought,
His mother would become distraught
And he would soon be caught!

OCELOTS

The nocturnal ocelots sleep for twelve to fourteen hours a day in thick vegetation on the ground, in hollow trees, or on tree branches. While the female ocelot sleeps in a different spot every day, once she gives birth to her kittens, she comes back to their birth den daily to care for them. Ocelots hunt at night, stalking rabbits, rodents, iguanas, or fish. They are also crepuscular, which means their greatest periods of activity are at dawn and dusk. Although ocelots are predators, they are also prey animals, hiding both from animals they want to eat and from animals that want to eat them.

HOW THE SLOTH SLEEPS

Green algae grows upon her back.
She eats a little for a snack
And sleeps all day above the ground
Upside down, just hanging around.

At night she'll climb with two-toed feet
While looking for some leaves to eat.
She hides and chews without a sound
Upside down, just hanging around.

Once a week, she will descend
Hoping not to meet her end.
She'll do her business on the ground
(But not for long, no hanging around!)

When she's done, she'll climb a tree
Leisurely and gracefully.
I think you know where she'll be found–
Upside down, just hanging around.

TWO-TOED SLOTHS

Found in the Amazon rainforest, nocturnal two-toed sloths can sleep up to sixteen hours a day, often while hanging upside down from a tree branch. Sloths also like to sleep curled up in a ball in the fork of a tree. At night, two-toed sloths wake and eat leaves. Because the leaves give them very little energy or muscle tone, sloths must conserve energy by moving slowly and hardly ever leaving their trees. They go to the ground just once a week to defecate. This is a risky time for them because they are too slow to flee from predators. Sloths are one of the slowest-moving animals on Earth, with a top speed of about .15 miles per hour. They are so inactive that algae actually grows on their backs, providing them with a food source and camouflaging them by making their fur appear green. Thanks to their extremely long and strong claws, sloths can eat, sleep, mate, and even die while hanging upside down.

DOGFISH SHARKS WHO SLEEP AND SWIM

These sharks can't breathe
Unless they're moving.
Water isn't
Merely soothing.

Rather, it is
Used for breathing,
Flowing over gills,
And leaving
Some of us
To stop and think,

"These dogfish never
sleep a wink."

"Aren't they tired?"
You might ask.
It turns out they
Can multitask!

Because their spines
Can navigate,
These sharks don't
Have to stay awake.

Their lives would
Certainly be grim
If dogfish couldn't
Sleep and swim.

SPINY DOGFISH SHARKS

Some shark species need to keep swimming forward to survive. This forward movement pushes the oxygen-rich water through their mouths and over their gills, allowing them to breathe. One might think that since these sharks need to keep moving, perhaps it is impossible for them to sleep. Scientists are not sure whether all sharks sleep, but studies have shown that the spiny dogfish shark navigates with its spine, which allows it to sleep off and on while swimming. When sleeping, cloudy membranes cover their open eyes.

A FLAMBOYANCE
OF FLAMINGOS

A flamboyance of flamingos will slumber in a lake
How fabulous that every bird can have a feather bed!
(But if eagles start to circle, then they may stay half awake.)
A flamboyance of flamingos will slumber in a lake.

They'll stand upon a slender leg, until they need a break,
Elegantly shifting to the other leg instead.
A flamboyance of flamingos will slumber in a lake,
How fabulous that every bird can have a feather bed!

FLAMINGOS

A flock of flamingos, also known as a flamboyance, can vary in size from just a few flamingos up to a million! Flamingos often sleep in shallow water while standing on one leg, nestling the other leg underneath them for warmth. Balancing on one leg requires the least muscle tone for flamingos, allowing them to save energy. When the standing leg eventually tires, they will switch to the other leg without waking up. Flamingos curve their necks backward and rest their heads on their feathers while sleeping.

When they feel threatened, flamingos will sleep with one eye open. The half of the brain opposite from the open eye remains awake, while the other half of the brain is asleep. This type of sleep (known as unihemispheric sleep), allows them to watch for predators such as lions, cheetahs, and eagles who might want to eat their eggs or young.

DUCKS IN A ROW

Ducks in a row
Ducks in a row

What do you know
About ducks in a row?

Those in the middle
Are fast asleep

But the outside ducks
Can't sleep too deep.

They must have one eye
Open wide
To spot those
Predators who hide

Hungry
Waiting
Lying low

Hoping to eat
Those ducks in a row.

MALLARD DUCKS

Mallard ducks are diurnal, remaining active during the day and sleeping at night. They sleep close to eleven hours, often on the water, where they feel safest. They also often sleep in a row, with the ducks on the inside of the line fully asleep. The two ducks on the ends of the line are in a state of unihemispheric sleep, keeping their outside eye open, while the half of their brains opposite the outside eye remains awake. This allows them to spot predators, such as foxes, skunks,

FRIGATE BIRD SLEEPS
ON THE WING

Frigate fishes
From the sky,
Swooping toward
The fish who fly.

Above the sea for
Miles and miles –
When frigate hunts
It takes a while.

Surfing thermals
While she sleeps,
Under clouds
For weeks and weeks.

Her head droops
Just a bit tonight.
Does frigate
Dream while
She's in flight?

FRIGATE BIRDS

Frigate birds can fly for months at a time over the ocean while hunting for flying fish. Because of their badly webbed feet and poorly waterproofed feathers, they cannot rest on the water. Instead, they glide on pockets of rising air for up to forty miles without flapping their wings.

In 2016, scientists from the Max Planck Institute for Ornithology proved for the first time that frigate birds can sleep while flying. During the day, they hunt for fish, but at night, they nap for a few minutes. Most of the time, these naps happen during unihemispheric sleep, where the frigates rest one half of their brains while keeping the other half alert. However, they sometimes experience bihemispheric sleep where both halves of the bird's brain turn off at the same time, allowing the frigates to have a few seconds of REM sleep. During these periods, the birds do not drop out of the

THE LEMURS' JOURNEY TO MADAGASCAR

For those who left by accident
So many million years ago,
How many hazy weeks were spent
Captive to the current's flow?

So many million years ago
Quiet, resting while at sea,
Captive to the current's flow,
While drifting on a fallen tree.

Quiet, resting while at sea,
(The ceaseless blue, the starry nights)
While drifting on a fallen tree.
When they awoke – a paradise!

The ceaseless blue, the starry nights,
How many hazy weeks were spent?
When they awoke, a paradise
For those who left by accident.

ANCIENT LEMURS

Scientists believe that lemurs may have accidentally "rafted" from the east coast of Africa to the island of Madagascar forty to fifty million years ago. Storms may have washed hibernating lemurs out to sea on rafts made of dense vegetation or fallen trees. Their journey of three hundred miles probably took at least three weeks. When they arrived, they found themselves in a paradise with many natural resources and few predators.

While seventeen species of lemurs are now extinct, one hundred and eleven species and subspecies can still be found in Madagascar and some tiny neighboring islands. These lemurs differ greatly from each other in many ways, including sleep patterns. While many are nocturnal or diurnal, others, such as the mongoose lemur, are cathemeral and can be active during the day or

THE BRAINLESS JELLYFISH

This jellyfish will often glide
Then flip so that her underside
Is facing upward toward the sun.
She'll grow a meal
And when she's done,
She'll eat the greens that she has grown
And fall asleep
All on her own.

It isn't easy to explain
How she's so smart
without a brain.

THE UPSIDE-DOWN JELLYFISH

Upside-down jellyfish are ancient organisms without brains. Instead, their nervous system is a simple web of nerve cells that extends throughout their bodies, called a nerve net. They like to spend a lot of time upside down in shallow water, pulsating, and waving their lacy underparts vertically. This exposes the algae in their tissues to the sun and allows it to grow. The jellyfish will then absorb energy and nutrients from the algae. Recent experiments at the California Institute of Technology have shown that jellyfish have times when their pulsating slows and they appear to sleep. They can be woken if they are disturbed but will still be groggy. Scientists need to study the apparent sleep patterns of jellyfish further. However, if jellyfish can sleep, it may mean that sleep evolved very early on for animals and is not only necessary for complex brains, but also for simple nervous systems.

A SONGBIRD
DREAMS OF SINGING

You'll hear him in the early hours
Singing while inspecting flowers
Or after thunderstorms and showers
When worms aren't hard to find.

Other birds may dream of worms
Or flower beds or thunderstorms
But every night this bird performs
A concert in his mind.

He tries to make his song unique.
He'll dream of when to dip and peak.
When daylight comes he'll part his beak
And sing what he designed.

Other birds may dream of worms
Or flower beds or thunderstorms
But in his dreams this bird performs
A song, each night refined.

ZEBRA FINCHES

Many scientists believe that because birds and mammals go through cycles of REM sleep, they are capable of dreaming. Scientists also have evidence that some animals relive the events of their day while sleeping, such as laboratory mice who practise going through mazes in their sleep. Although it is unproven, it might also be possible that some birds dream of such things as storms, worms, and flying. In the case of songbirds, scientists at the University of Chicago have done studies on zebra finches demonstrating that the males practise and refine their songs while dreaming, adding little flourishes to make their version of the song unique. Zebra finches are diurnal birds who rest in the afternoon and sleep for about ten hours a night. Like many other songbirds, when they awake in the morning, they sing with particular enthusiasm in what is known as the dawn chorus.

THE DESERT SNAIL
THAT AWOKE TO FAME

(An Account From
Those Who Knew Him)

Nobody at the museum could tell
That he was alive inside his shell.
Glued to a board and given a label,
He tried to escape, but just wasn't able.

What could he do? He took a long nap,
Which lasted for almost four years, in fact.
When we finally noticed a bit of his slime,
We knew he'd been resting a very long time!

"He's alive!" we agreed. "We'll unglue him right now!"
We bathed him in water, which must have allowed
This snail to awake from his long aestivation
To lots of attention and much admiration.

(Can you imagine his total surprise
Awaking to so many curious eyes?)
Placed in a jar and supplied with food,
He posed for his portrait, once he was unglued.

We think he deserves an apology
From those of us here in Conchology
At the British Museum, that's world-renowned,
Where he patiently waited, until he was found.

THE DESERT SNAIL

In 1846, the British Museum in London added a snail shell from the Egyptian desert to its collection. The conchologists, who study the shells of animals, mistakenly assumed that the shell was empty. In fact, the shell was inhabited by a snail who was still very much alive. Once captive, it began aestivating, which is a state of inactivity that snails enter when the weather is too hot or dry. (In the desert, these snails burrow underground, sealing themselves in their shells with their own slime. Some may even aestivate for up to three years!)

In 1850, museum conchologists noticed a slimy mucus plug underneath the shell and realized that the snail might still be alive. After the shell was bathed in warm water, the snail emerged. It became so famous for its long nap that the artist Annie Newman Waterhouse drew its portrait. Today, its shell can still be seen at the Museum of Natural History in London. Although accounts from the 1850s refer to this snail as a male, desert snails have both male and female sex organs and are actually hermaphrodites.

THE SPRING PEEPER

If this fine amphibian
Were found in the Caribbean
He wouldn't need to hibernate.
He'd be in quite another state –

Relaxing on a leaf or log
Just like the merry whistling frog.
Instead, he knows that he might freeze
If frost creeps in to bite the trees.

However, in the spring he'll thaw,
No worse for wear. We are in awe
Of peeper who can lift his head
And peep, returning from the dead.

SPRING PEEPERS

Spring peepers are nocturnal frogs found in Canada and the United States. They live in grassy lowlands and wooded areas near ponds or swamps. In the winter, they hibernate under trees or logs. If the temperature dips below thirty-two degrees Fahrenheit, seventy percent of a peeper's body will freeze, their heart will stop pumping, and they will appear to be dead. Luckily, a substance known as glycerol prevents deadly ice crystals from forming in the blood. When hibernating, cloudy membranes will cover their open eyes. Come spring, the peepers will thaw, and the males will start peeping, hoping to attract females.

THE QUEENS TAKE NINETY NAPS EACH DAY

The queens take ninety naps each day,
Piled together in a heap.
A drowsy synchronized ballet,
Workers toil so queens can sleep.

Piled together in a heap,
Mouths are closed, antennae shake.
Workers toil so queens can sleep.
Why should royals stay awake?

Mouths are closed, antennae shake,
Thoughts converge and float downstream.
Why should royals stay awake?
Workers toil so queens can dream.

Thoughts converge and float downstream –
A drowsy synchronized ballet.
Workers toil so queens can dream.
The queens take ninety naps each day.

THE WORKER ANT'S POWER NAP

You didn't know, perhaps,
That this ant takes power naps.

It's quite a short collapse.
(Sixty seconds will elapse.)

How many naps will there be?
About two hundred and fifty-three.

FIRE ANTS

Ants live in highly organized societies known as colonies where every member is assigned a job. The queen lays eggs, the male drones fertilize the eggs, and the female worker ants handle all other tasks, such as taking care of the young, building and maintaining the ant home, and finding food. While some ant colonies have only one queen, the fire ant colony has three. A fire ant queen takes ninety naps a day for six minutes each, sleeping for a total of about nine hours per day. The queens also synchronize their naps, piling on top of each other when asleep and then separating when awake. The worker ants must get by on around two hundred and fifty-three one-minute power naps, which adds up to about four and a half hours of sleep per day.

The queens have two states of sleep: when their mouths are open and their antennae are half raised, they are in a light sleep; when their antennae are folded, and their mouths are shut, they are in a deeper sleep. Sometimes, their antennae start to quiver in this deeper state. This rapid antennae movement is thought to be similar to REM sleep, leading some scientists to believe that queen ants can also dream. Because queens have such an easy life, they can live up to six years. Worker ants are not so lucky, living only six months to a year.

GLOSSARY

AMPHIBIAN: a cold-blooded animal with a spine. Amphibians breathe with gills when they are forming and then typically with lungs when they are adults.

BIHEMISPHERIC SLEEP: sleeping with both halves of the brain at the same time

CACKLE: the collective noun used for a group of hyenas

CATHEMERAL ANIMALS: those animals who are irregularly active both during the day and night

CONCHOLOGIST: those who study the shells of mollusks, such as shellfish and snails

CREPUSCULAR ANIMALS: those animals who are most active during the twilight hours of dawn and dusk

DIURNAL ANIMALS: those animals who are most active during the day

FLAMBOYANCE: a collective noun used for a group of flamingos

HIBERNATION: a resting state in which the body temperature drops and the metabolism slows drastically. Hibernation is a different state than sleep.

MAMMAL: a warm-blooded animal with a spine. The females give birth to live young and feed them milk.

NOCTURNAL ANIMALS: those animals who are most active at night

PREDATOR: an animal that eats other animals

PREY: an animal that is eaten by other animals

POD: a collective noun used for a group of whales

REM SLEEP: a state of sleep during which the animal has rapid eye movements, an overall loss of muscle tone with occasional muscle jerks and twitches, and faster breathing. The brain activity during REM sleep is similar to that seen while the animal is awake. A human in REM sleep will usually experience vivid dreams with plots, characters, emotions, and sensory imagery.

UNIHEMISPHERIC SLEEP: sleep where one half of the brain is awake, with the opposite eye usually remaining open

ACKNOWLEDGMENTS

I would like to thank the following people
for their guidance and support:

Jonathan Ablett, Natural History Museum, London, United Kingdom

Claire Bedbrook, California Institute of Technology, Pasadena, California, United States

Marina Blanco, Duke Lemur Center, Duke University, Chapel Hill, North Carolina, United States

Dr. Eric Chudler, Center for Sensorimotor Neural Engineering at the University of Washington, United States

Sarah Clark, Duke Lemur Center, Duke University, Chapel Hill, North Carolina, United States

Stephanie Fennessy, Giraffe Conservation Foundation, Namibia

Dr. James P. Gibbs, Department of Conservation and Biology, SUNY-ESF, Syracuse, New York, United States

Jenisa Leagnavar, Shedd Aquarium, Chicago, Illinois, United States

Dr. Gary M. Lovett, Cary Institute of Ecosystem Studies, Millbrook, New York, United States

Sy Montgomery, author and naturalist, Hancock, New Hampshire, United States

Dr. Craig Packer, Lion Research Center, University of Minnesota, Minneapolis, United States

Dr. Erik Patel, Lemur Conservation Foundation, Cornell University, Ithaca, New York, United States

Dr. Niels Rattenborg, Max Planck Institute for Ornithology, Seewiesen, Germany

And a special thanks to:

Sofija Canavan, Margoliash Laboratory,
University of Chicago MSTP for her guidance, patience, and generosity.